MW01076136

Wander(lust)

JASMINE MAH

 leaf
publishing
house

Dedication

For Dad and Grandpa Jack, until we meet again.

Introduction

The book you have in your hands is unique. Though every book is different in its own way, I promise this one is most unusual. Before you start, imagine stumbling upon a faded photograph. The kind that flutter out while you're sifting through piles of old lists and bills and scraps of paper bearing long-forgotten names and phone numbers. It falls at your feet and you bend down to pick it up. The edges are slightly curled upwards, the colors not as vivid as they once were, and the people not as young. In that instant, you are holding a memory in your hand, just as you are at this very moment. The only difference is that this book is a collection of snapshots captured by words rather than a camera. Most are based on true events that happened to someone, maybe to me or perhaps to you. Think of them as miniature flashbacks to first and last kisses, to the hellos and goodbyes, to the exhilaration of the departures gate and the comfort of coming home again, and to all those moments in-between that make life what it is - a journey worthy of wanderlust. This is a love letter to all the dreamers and romantics scattered across the world. May you live one thousand and one lives and look back on them with the same nostalgia that is written in these pages.

A Thousand Lives

Do you ever think that you could have lived a thousand different lives, all at the same time? I left pieces of my heart in every new city that I dragged my MEC backpack through. I re-stitched that Canadian flag on the side so often that I carried a needle and red and white thread in my pocket. By the time I arrived in Italy, my heart had been broken in pieces, and I didn't think even a shard remained. I had lived through many lifetimes during the evenings. My hand out the window of a bright blue VW with early 2000s German rap playing in one ear and the tickle of an accent in the other. At 2am, I lay awake in a flat filled with French books and posters of films I've never seen, somewhere near the best spätzle joint in Berlin precisely 7233km from home. There, I'd think to myself: this could be your life. But it wasn't. Because my wild, wild heart, the broken one, wanted other beings in other forlorn dots on the map. So I followed her like a reckless lost girl, and we went to Paris and kissed tombstones with red Chanel lipstick, we slept off vodka as the train rattled across the black Siberian midnight. We danced until my clothes were drenched in Costa Rica; pretended to speak Spanish in taxis and bit into mangoes fresh from the tree on the streets of Kathmandu. The Himalayas were watching our every move. In all of that recklessness, the foreign faces touched with my eyes, with my lips, we lived. I lived those thousand lives. Then I brought the only piece of my heart to Italy, tired and dull, and a boy thought it was enough and it was. One thousand and one.

A Sunday Kind of Love

I want a Sunday kind of love. When Saturday nights' flawlessly applied makeup is smeared on one of those throwaway wipes and my hair is a mess, and we will guiltlessly spend all morning in sweatpants in bed. I'll wear your college T-shirt with the faded "H" and the tiny hole on the right shoulder, you'll wear a smile. You'll be scruffy even though you shaved the night before. They linger on your skin, the smoke from the bar and one too many whiskey sours and my Gucci perfume. The air outside will be crisp like the falling leaves, a Sunday in November going on Thanksgiving perhaps. But I'll be warmly wrapped up with you in the rumpled cotton sheets, fingers curled around my favorite Seattle mug, the one with the tiny chip you glued back on. I'll be blowing on the hot coffee with little puffs while you tuck pieces of hair behind my ear, moving it all to one side to kiss my neck and make me shiver despite the heat in my hands. I'll implore you to read me Neruda from my dog-eared copy of Love Poems, "I want to do with you what spring does with the cherry trees," but poetry doesn't suit your lips that are more at home when they move on mine than they are reciting the foreign words of another man.

Mulberries in Sicily

I had never eaten a mulberry before that steamy afternoon at the market in Catania. I had to look up the English translation afterward, I didn't even know what a mulberry was. A fictional thing perhaps, a figment of nursery rhymes and stories told by grey-haired grandfathers on front porches. In my imagination, mulberries belonged in a Nicholas Sparks novel. There would be a brimming bowl of mulberries on a table somewhere in South Carolina, waiting to be nibbled upon on a fated night with fated lovers. We bought them from a boy who was tiny for his age, his eyes eerily out of proportion with the rest of his body. You might describe them as pleading, but I saw them as they were- exuberant. He very carefully let them tumble from the tattered basket into a paper bag, swiftly picking up the ones stuck on the bottom one by one. Overly attentive, as if the inky blackberries were diamonds, only he could see. I ate my first mulberry there on the street, surrounded by the sounds of a Sicilian summer. A baby cried. A car crashed. Horns blared, and pans clattered. Steam hissed, and a zuppa di pesce gurgled and overflowed onto the stovetop. Someone cursed. Someone prayed. I didn't expect to taste what I did. My head was full of sounds and the sharp, acrid metallic smell of fish and freshly-shucked oysters. Maybe he fed me the first one, I don't remember well. All I remember is the fat berry pressed up against my lips, plump, velvety, and warm from the sun. I resisted at first, this strange fruit without a name being forced on me. But I took it, pressed it with my tongue to the roof of my mouth until it finally burst. It was the best thing I'd ever tasted, like sunshine and forbidden love and the adjective "plush," sweet and comforting and somehow erotic in nature. I had to close my eyes so I wouldn't feel naked in the market. I had never eaten a mulberry before.

The Morning After

I wake slowly, blinkingly. I have slept the sleep that boasts of the bottled ruby red Montepulciano sun from last night; the blackberries, wildflowers and sweet spices, the haze of jetlag, the checkered tablecloth, and a vague memory of the melody to Moon River still playing in my head. It is autumn in New York. The season of change. Gilded leaves litter Central Park, crunchy underfoot, the biting morning air that heeds to the warmth of the sun. We arrived yesterday afternoon, stumbling off a dark flight filled with milanesi and right out into the bright lights of the city that never sleeps. Dice is what came to mind. Like a pair were thrown out onto the craps table, the eyes of everyone on the fate of two insignificant, tiny objects. I hear the whispered pleas that 'luck be a lady.' "Sfortuna al gioco, fortuna in amore" is what the Italians say. Unlucky at cards, lucky in love, but not both. You can never have both.

There's a red lipstick smear across my pillow. I think about the traces I left on the wine glass, the starched bleach-white napkin, and on his cheek. Maybe other places too. A monogram. Another passport stamp. I was here. This was mine, for a night, for a fleeting moment. For a fleeting moment, we were lovers atop the Empire State, poets on Canal and Bowery, Hemingway in a dive bar, and rebels without a cause. Sunshine is pouring in through the curtains, casting shards of light and lightness that dance across his back. New York beckons but the air in this hotel room on the fifth floor is thick with sleep, regret, and him. Him.

The slow rise and fall of his chest, naked against the white sheets. I hear his breath, heavy and slow, I don't turn over to look, but I can picture his almost-black hair on the pillow, the sharp angles of a jawline in stark contrast to the soft, down duvet and its rounded corners. If you knew me like you think you do, you'd know his eyes are green. I've only ever had two vices, smoking, and green-eyed men. I haven't smoked since the new year, but I refuse to renounce the second. The warmth of the bed is enveloping, tempting, and teasing. I'm reminded of last night. The faintest headache, a sea of emerald green, the just-woken deepness in his voice and unshaven cheek tickling my shoulders, they all try to keep me here, but I slip out and start the shower. It's too late to tangle the sheets, to linger in languid kisses and questions, the day awaits. I rub what's left of the red lipstick off my lips, smearing it across my face and the back of my hand.

We walk hand in hand, his free hand wrapped around a paper coffee cup with those plastic lids you can't fully trust. He never drinks American coffee. The only time he does is in New York as if this city changes things- me, you, him, here we don't exist. Here, he drinks coffee in a takeaway cup and holds my hand and lingers and laughs. We don't exist on these streets, and if we don't exist, I suppose this never happened.

Rooftops and Rome

It was sometime in summer, let's call it a midsummer's night. Rome was suffocating with the kind of heat that emanates from every single cobblestone and ruin of the city, after a long, hot day of pure sunshine. It's that season when everyone and everything in the city is a little more provocative- the hemlines rise, shoulders and collarbones are exposed to the night air, hair is let down and then gathered back up, and imaginations run rampant. Rome will do things to you like call at midnight to dance on rooftops. And you'd have to decline at first politely, that's what ladies do. But you'll already be thinking of that red dress, backless and hanging with high expectations, and how perfect it would go with his eyes. You resist. It's late, and you should really be up early the next day. Things to check off lists and all that. But then the Roman accent is persuasive, not by force but by nature, and it doesn't take long before you're whispering "arrivo", I'm coming, and slipping out the door, through the night, and thinking about those few seconds when you shiver, not from the air but from where his lips were. They say Rome is meant to be lived on rooftops. I think it's meant to be lived in the in-between, the dash, the dot, dot, dot... like those moments right before you see each other across the lit piazza when the tension and anticipation are so high that all you can hear is the sound of your own heartbeat and the voices of all your friends back home asking how could you possibly fall for him. Italian, from Rome, and far too gorgeous for monogamy, isn't that how they are? Maybe. You feel his eyes on you before you actually see him, on your back and the nape of your neck. It's just for tonight, just for this summer you'll tell yourself, as you turn around.

Strangers in Switzerland

I was nineteen and naive when we met in a hostel lobby one drizzly morning in Zurich. I had bedhead that only looks alluring when you're nineteen, wearing wool socks and loudly munching on cereal while gulping it down with what seemed like a gallon of ice cold Swiss milk. I remember thinking I had never tasted anything like it before. Thinking back to my first time in Switzerland, the few things I remember having to do with milk, chocolate, and a boy. It was the kind of day I would have happily crawled back into the bunk beds with a book, but his eyes convinced me otherwise. They were blue, not my personal preference to tell the truth, but somehow they seemed to bring the sky to me on that grey afternoon. We decided to take the first tram to the last stop of the line. He was the Ethan Hawke to my Julie Delpy, and we talked and didn't talk for hours, our feet propped up on the seats in front of us like the kids that we were. And with the rain pounding on the roof of the tram, I thought about perfect strangers. All the perfect strangers I had met along the way, kissed along the way. I thought about how perfect strangers can change your life. Somewhere along the track, he told me he was in love with a girl from Canada, and I knew that he was thinking of her while he looked at me, as if me being from the same country was like having a piece of her back. We talked about missed chances and about chasing love. The rain let up. By the time we reached the last stop, he had decided to do the chase for real, and I was euphoric, enraptured, enchanted. Not because of an entire day on a Swiss tram with a boy with the bluest eyes, but because I was there when a perfect stranger decided to take a risk for love.

One Day in Positano

I'm woken from my Lambrusco-induced sleep by the sound of Lorenzo attempting to balance a tray filled with cappuccinos, cream-filled brioches, and hand-squeezed spremuta from Sicilian blood oranges as he walks precariously towards me. The juice looks like a sunset in a glass, and he looks like a dream.

I'd found him the other day in the middle of the Mediterranean. I was swimming, and he was fishing shirtless. The latter of which is my new favorite hobby. Lorenzo doesn't speak English, which suits him perfectly seeing as he wants to do everything but talk. He has eyes the color of my home; the dark forest green of pine trees that cover Alberta's Rocky Mountains, with flecks of amber as if someone had splashed a bit of Italian sunshine into them.

It's the height of summer in Italy, the air thick with a certain kind of wanting that emerges at this time of year. I'm languishing in a morning stupor, the cotton sheets draped over me and off the California king. Lorenzo has drawn the bath on the veranda, so I take my brioche in one hand and grab him in the other. I step out into a cloudless blue sky with the rainbow colors of Positano beneath us. We spend another hour soaking in the bubbles and each other until the church bells start to chime below us, signaling that we are already late to our lunch date in town. I throw on my favorite white cotton dress from Antica Sartoria and strappy sandals that are entirely impractical for Positano's winding cobblestone paths. He's in full white linen, the kind of outfit that every woman adores but so few men can actually pull off unless they were born by the sea. My still-wet hair is hanging down my back, and I can feel the tickle of the beads of water as they slip down my spine. The mid-day sun will dry it in no time, so we head out, Lorenzo's bronzed arm hanging lazily over my shoulders. Lunch is at Chez Black, and I order spaghetti ai ricci di mare because they bring it in a dish shaped like a sea-urchin and I've always loved the spectacle it creates as the waiter lifts the cover. I practically drown myself in the Frizzantino, and I am nursing euphoric drunkenness when our group decides to take a boat out for the afternoon. We laze the day away on the yacht between swims and impromptu kisses while the sun scorches the coastline.

Back at the apartment, Lorenzo puts himself to work on dinner as I wash the sea and the day away. I leave the salt in my hair though, because nothing can imitate the waves from a day spent in the water. Candles light the entire terrazzo, competing with the stars on this clear night. There's something about the way that Italian men look at you, isn't there? As if there is nowhere else they would rather be than caught in a moment with you. Lorenzo is tracing Italian words on my back, telling me to guess each one. Bellissima. Perfetta. Ti voglio. I intentionally get the last one wrong because I know if I say it aloud, the night of dancing that awaits us will never come to fruition. I pull him out into the midnight, and we make our way towards the music and the stars.

Love Letter to Italy

You were like the captain of the football team, such a stereotypical choice that I wanted to avoid making, that I had to avoid making. It's almost shameful to utter the words "I fell in love with Italy" however, I suppose I should have considered that I used to be a cheerleader and therefore you were my inescapable fate from the start. I'll come right out and say that it was lust at first sight and not love. It was not love for a long time because of your beauty. Captivating, impossible to ignore or deny. That summer, I was in awe of you. You made me marvel before I knew the word. You were the most beautiful thing I had ever seen. Wide-eyed, I took to your cobblestone streets, negotiating the path of Gods and lesser gods in high-heels and dodging glances from your entourage, dark-eyed and tempting. But it wasn't them I was looking at, neither the men nor the women. Seductive as they are, I couldn't take my eyes off you and you alone. You have that kind of hold on people, and dare I say it, on virgins especially. First-timers. Yet the more I came to you, entranced and enthralled, the more I realized that amongst your beauty there were ruins. I began to see your faults because we all have them. Not even you are perfect; actually, you are the farthest thing from perfection. You hide behind this façade of slow dinners out in the piazza at twilight, the laughter of friends over clinking glasses filled to the brim with Aperol, prosecco, soda water and ice, the cypress-lined drives in the Tuscan countryside, a wake of white dust following a red 1960 Alfa Romeo Giulietta, a silent prayer after wine-fueled nights of passion in a language created for courtship and opera.

Your façade is literally in the façade of buildings that not only house history but are history themselves. You seduce easily, using all these things as part of your armory, but you let only a select few in. I get it, I've done it too. It's a self-preservation thing. So many have thought they loved you until they saw you without makeup in the morning, with fluorescent lighting after a sleepless night when nothing is going right, and everything in the world is wrong. Full of secrets and corruption, of bureaucratic failures and few everyday successes. You like to dwell on the past, your past conquests, your past glories. You live in the past, but this isn't high school anymore, and it's like everyone grew up around you. You're vain as well. Sometimes too arrogant to admit your faults but depending on the day, you're self-deprecating at the same time, quick to react and slow to change. The others, they want only the beauty without the beast. But Italy, my dearest, you are both. A paradox of sorts and a riddle that can never be solved. And only a handful of us are content with an unsolved riddle, with getting lost and losing ourselves in it. Some people might say that a love like ours is destructive. I say it's the only kind to live for. Where I am so entwined and tangled up in you that I can't discern where you start, and I end up. To live with you is to be you and to know that on some days, there are ruins in our beauty and that on other days, there is beauty in ruins. You've taught me not only about love but of life. I left behind so much for you, sacrificed everything that I thought of as sacred before you came along. But in you, I finally found what is sacred: slow dinners out in the piazza, twilight, the laughter of friends, the cypress-lined drives, Tuscan countryside, a wake of white dust, a red Alfa Romeo, wine-fueled nights, a language, courtship, opera, and most of all and in it all, passion.

Airport Arrivals

Luggage-less, I walked up to the sliding doors and blinked as I felt the sudden whoosh of air against my face. When I opened them again, I was standing in front of this familiar stranger. A look and a smile that I knew from a different world when our surroundings were my comfort zone, and the language were my own. I kissed him, which is a bold move after you've been traveling for over 14 hours but seems almost obligatory at airport arrivals. If not for yourself, then to add to the romance of it all for everyone else. He tasted like beer; I remember it distinctly. Poor thing had been waiting for over an hour past my estimated arrival, and he ended up passing the time by drinking. I still have a hunch that it was also partly to calm his nerves because if they were like mine, they were probably off the charts. My heart was beating out of my chest, the kind of beating where you become subconscious that the people around you can actually hear it. Unless you have been in my position, one-half of a long-distance relationship. It's hard to describe the sensation of being in the presence of a person whose pixelated face you know like the back of your hand, but that is entirely foreign in flesh and blood. Our relationship in the last few months was solely reliant on Skype and emails, and in this way, you form an intense emotional connection. But face-to-face, I could feel a disconnect between the physical and emotional. I needed to bridge that disconnect immediately, so I took my shaking hand and gripped his, and together we walked out of the airport and into the Italian night. It seems bizarre, but it felt like coming home. When I finally pulled back the covers to sleep that night, there was a handwritten note from him on the pillow: Benvenuta a casa piccola. Welcome home little one.

Tanqueray and You

I can't drink Tanqueray anymore without thinking of you. Sometimes I sit in Upper East Side bars, the beautiful faces of strangers lit by candlelight and the false promises of a Saturday night in the city, and I catch a glimpse of it, the dark green glinting glass. That bottle that we shared. It was an Indian summer, and we were sitting next to the river, you and I and Tanqueray. I couldn't look at you or the fire in your eyes. Your eyes that held mine, one second too long. They were green like the glass of that iconic bottle, an impossible color to be honest, but we were full of impossibilities. We were sixteen, and we thought we knew everything. I can't drink Tanqueray without feeling your hands in my hair, our clothes smelling of smoke and our kisses full of juniper, coriander, angelica, and licorice. We drank the whole bottle that night, passing it back and forth, each sip adding to the intimacy of it all. Imagining your lips pressed to mine and not the neck of that bottle. I can't drink Tanqueray without thinking of our high school hallways, red and gold, pep rallies, Dashboard Confessional, and final exams. Nobody here can live forever, quiet in the grasp of dusk and summer. And just like that graduation came and we shook hands and left illegible letters in each other's yearbooks. What you wrote to me, I've never read. It's there for the day when I will finally drink Tanqueray again and smile and remember what it was like to be sixteen and in love with the world at our feet, when we knew everything and nothing.

Screw Soulmates

I don't believe in soulmates. I've always loved the idea, but I know they aren't real. I have been all around the world, and I can see them in every city I've ever explored. I close my eyes, and I'm hand-in-hand with an investment broker on Wall Street, avid, thirsty, and career-driven with ecru pantsuits, understated statement pieces and a closet full of last season's Jimmy Choos. Then there's me with a broke artist living a kind of penniless perfection in Williamsburg, eating greasy Chinese takeout with yesterday's chopsticks. I would wear overalls and plastic-rimmed glasses and braided crowns for days at a time, and I'd be euphorically happy. He'd paint my portraits and the portraits of other girls. Then we'd get in screaming, paint-throwing arguments and then make the kind of messy love that is art itself. Or I could have stayed in Berlin for more than one night. Stayed with that trilingual German boy who wore scarves and thrift-store leather jackets with such ease, spent our evenings attending French poetry slams and doing whatever young, European intellectuals do. Which probably involves getting high on weed and philosophical ideations. But then what if I had stayed in the country I was born in, married a wheat farmer and sipped sweet tea on wraparound porches, wrapped in flannel plaid blankets.

I would have been happy there as much as in Berlin and Williamsburg and Wall Street because I'm sure my soul was never looking for its mate. It was just seeking the past life it remembered the most, and what it could never forget, despite a thousand lives, was the warmth of the Italian sun and the arms of a green-eyed, olive-skinned boy with the Mediterranean in his dark hair and in his veins.

Up in the Air

I rushed onto the plane in three-inch wedges, a flowery yellow wrap dress that was near-falling-off, and a Kate Spade crab purse trailing behind me. My hair was stuck to the sweat on my neck, and I was anything but the picture of grace at that moment. I had just caught the last flight to Milan from Toronto by a few minutes, and when I went to find my seat, 33A, to my surprise, a young boy was sitting there.

"I think you're in my spot," I said all at once in an exhale.

He just stared at me. I knew I was quite the sight, but I couldn't help but think that he hadn't understood me. He had that look of utter confusion about him, so I just gestured to my seat and then to myself, and he immediately jumped up without saying a word.

I have this guilty pleasure whenever I travel, and it's to guess where people are from and then why they are going where they're going, all before we've exchanged any actual words. For whatever reason, I pegged this one as an Italian going home. There are just ways I can tell now, I can't explain how. It's not even that this boy looked classically Italian--he had sandy blond hair, a slight build, wide eyes, and was dressed more like an American with a sweatshirt, shorts, and black Nikes on his feet--he could have been anything but Italian if my deductions were made on looks alone. Yet over the years, I've acquired something else, a sixth sense you might say, in identifying Italians. I think it has something to do with the way they look at you, without any shame or cognizance of crossing any social behavior barriers. Unwavering is the adjective.

I decided to test out my theory, so I accidentally kicked his backpack, said sorry in English, and waited for his response.

"Nothing," he responded. I immediately knew that I was right. He was Italian. In Italian, "niente" would be a typical automatic reply to a similar contextual situation and the translation is "nothing" whereas a native English speaker would use expressions such as "no problem" or "no worries." I smiled to myself, triumphant until realizing I was in that precarious situation of which language to use. I always think about how I hate to be spoken to in English when someone is aware that I can speak and understand Italian. So I always try to keep this in mind when talking to Italians, in this case, I stuck with English.

"Are you going home?" I asked.
"Yes," the boy replied with a timid smile.

"Do you live in Milan?" I prodded further.

"What? Can you repeat it?" he said, looking flustered. I took this chance to say something in Italian.

"Sei di Milano?" Are you from Milan?

"Oh, parli italiano? Perché?" he wondered out loud, his eyes opening wide with surprise.

"Abito a Bergamo," I explained. I live in Bergamo.

And so began the eight-hour plane trip over the Atlantic, an ocean that I've crossed innumerable times in the past ten years, but the first that I didn't sleep through. After I gave away my Italian, the boy who seemed so shy suddenly became the chattiest seatmate that I had ever encountered. He had just turned eighteen and gone abroad to Toronto to practice his English. Before returning home to enjoy his last real summer of freedom before his final year of liceo, high school. Something about him, his youth and innocence, reminded me of those high school years and of so many firsts. First love and everything that goes along with it. The kind of things you never forget. At one point, he told me about how he never understands when people talk to him in English. He was visibly nervous as the flight attendant made her way to our row to give us the tough decision of chicken or pasta for dinner.

"For me, pasta," he muttered when his turn came. Immediately after he turned to me and asked, "l'ho detto giusto?" Did I say it right?

I smiled and said, "sì, perfetto."

He smiled back with his eyes. Later on, he taught me the noun edilizia, construction. He asked more about Canada, I asked more about Italy.

We wrote our favorite Italian rap songs in each other's phones, me telling him about the lyrics in Mecna's "Non Ci Sei Più" where he references Lake Ontario:

Al Tramonto con due Bud ad Agosto sull' Ontario
dicesti "sai, voglio andare via da Milano, vuoi venire con me?"

At sunset, with two Buds in August on Lake Ontario
you said, "you know, I want to leave Milan, do you wanna come with me?"

And the romantic in me couldn't help but think how romantic this whole thing was. Two strangers raised in different cultures and languages, seated next to each other 35 000 feet in the air over an ocean, sharing a connection. Not romantic in its definition that would make my husband jealous, but romantic in its other meaning: of, characterized by, or suggestive of an idealized view of reality. These kinds of moments, they are my reality, and it is one that I have always wanted to have since my very first trip to Europe- the ability to sit next to a stranger, speak a foreign language, and laugh. I never in a million years would have thought that this idealized view of life, could, and would, become my own.

"Ce l'abbiamo fatta," he exclaimed as the plane soared over the Swiss Alps.

"We did it," I repeated. And we laughed, his brown eyes shining.

All the Sunsets

There's no manual for hearts. No cryptic, impossible-to-decipher IKEA-esque instructions that show you how to put the pieces back together, leaving you with an almost-heart, missing one screw causing it to sit slightly crooked in your chest cavity. I would take an imperfectly-assembled heart over the million and one pieces that feel like they've settled into the depths of my gut, sliding from side-to-side as I toss and turn in the pitch black of the night, seeming to come to life as my hand accidentally slips and touches the cold mattress where your heart used to be. This was all my doing, so I shouldn't even be writing this. The spilled milk is mine. I loved being in love with him, but at the same time, I couldn't keep loving him. His goodness was never meant for a woman like me. He needed white picket fences and freshly cut grass and Sunday mornings, I needed planes and Friday nights in Hong Kong. I was meant for little black dresses and nothing else. We were so happy until we weren't, so perfect until imperfection became what I craved. I knew I had to go. The fact was, I didn't love him more than all the sunsets in the world I hadn't yet seen. And so he called me selfish, called me adjectives and nouns that I never knew he knew. He called me crazy for choosing sunsets over a soul mate but what he didn't know what I never told him, is that my soul doesn't believe in monogamy.

She's promiscuous, a hot mess, flitting from city to city for one-night stands and falling in love all over the world.

Happier

Sometimes, in the middle of an ordinary day, I wonder where you are. What city you're in. What you're doing at this very moment. If your eyes are still that light green, like springtime. Of course, they are. Then I start thinking about how we almost had it all until you fucked everything up by falling out of love with us. The last time I saw you, we sat across from each other at that place we used to go to, the one right off campus with the cinnamon buns. It reminded me of innocence and of how we thought life would always be there in that café, on that street, in that city. We never imagined that I'd be here and you'd be wherever you are and that there would be a continent between us. I'm actually not sure about the continent part, but something in my bones tells me I'm probably right. I heard you found someone new. I've seen her shadow in photographs on Instagram. The curve of her back and the angles of her hand. I even know her smile, I have studied it trying to figure out what you said to make her laugh. I loved your wit, our banter, my dirty mouth, and how you'd kiss me hard to shut me up. She's beautiful, but you know that already. The worst part is that she's nothing like me, the first time I saw her blonde hair, I felt like a fraud. As if all that time, all those years, I had been nothing but her stand-in. Do you read her Pushkin and buy her your favorite books? I still have them, dog-eared to mark chapters that you used to love. It's those small things, the reminders of what we loved and lost. The folded pages, the first notes of a song, the smell of cinnamon, and spring.

I wonder if almost every boy in the world has bought more than one copy of his favorite book- one for you and one for her. The one that came after. The "could have been", and the "will be". The past and the future. I hate to admit it, but you look happier, you really do.

Whiskey

I hated showing up there with whiskey on my breath and that stupid smile on my red lips, but you had that intangible pull on me. Something invisible that could only be felt although people used to tell us that they could see it. I don't know why I showed up on your doorstep that Friday night, we'd been over for months by then and I didn't even have your number on my phone anymore. I'd purposely deleted it to avoid sending Jack Daniels'-fueled text messages that said "miss you" or some version of it. But your apartment number, the street name, those things were ingrained in my memory. As much as the ocean blue of your eyes, the feeling of your heart against mine and my back against the wall. You really shouldn't have opened the door, but you knew that we needed it, the surrendering. Oscar Wilde once said that the only way to get rid of temptation is to yield to it. So I did, and so did you. I yielded to the version of us I missed, the us that laughed entire nights away clutching our stomachs in agony to make it stop so we could breathe again. The us that could never get enough of the rush. You driving fast in the Nevada desert, my hair a mess and that kind of impossible feeling of being lost and found all at once.

That's the us I miss the most.

Call Me Baby

I used to hate it when my boyfriends would call me 'baby.' Don't call me that, I'd say. Don't call me 'baby.' Now I'm writing this four thousand miles from home, across the Atlantic Ocean where the boys don't speak my mother tongue, and they say things like bella, tesoro, and amore. And I loved it at first. The swirls of each familiar letter that placed side-by-side morphed into something so foreign and delectable, I couldn't help but fall. So fall in love I did. And the days became months that became years, and I became someone's treasure, someone's love, but little did I know, I would never again be someone's baby.

Italian doesn't use that term of endearment. You'll hear it but not with the heart. You'll hear it but not in that smooth, unrehearsed way that a native English speaker can use it with pure nonchalance and every cruel or honest intention in the book. So I tell myself there's nothing to mourn, nothing to miss. But there are still nights when I dream of that "unaccent," the one that belongs to a past life. The sound of a voice saying "hey baby" with an aspirated H that comes from a practiced mouth that grew up around a letter which doesn't exist here. This is such a small and insignificant thing, but there is also the stark realization that you can never know when the last time someone calls you baby will be. You can never know when the last time for anything will be. Maybe, just maybe, you'll move abroad, find yourself on a peninsula flanked by the Mediterranean and the Adriatic, and meet a boy, and it will dawn on you as it did me. You'll wake up in the pitch black of the night, and you won't remember the face of the last boy who could find "baby" in his vernacular, but his voice will somehow come back to you with perfect clarity. Sometimes I worry that it's not the word I mourn, but the life that could have been had I planted roots rather than grew wings. I worry about missing out on that life where I was someone's "baby" and not someone's "amore."

The Butterfly Effect

I'm laying on my back looking up at the sky, letting the first spring rain run mascara and tears down the sides of my face so that they slide over and under and seem to pool in my ears. Tiny black rain drops. A quick spectacular moment, I try to tell myself. The sensation makes me want to laugh out loud even though I'm crying, like when the sun is shining on a rainy day. It happens, you know, in the tropics. It can be raining and sunny at the same time, go figure. That's what I feel like now, like weather that can't make up its mind. It's impossible to know how much I'm crying, the briny tears mixing with the rain provides solace to my sense of pride. I've concluded that's why people cry in the shower because the falling water makes it impossible to quantify just how many tears you've spilled for another human being and the invisible sound waves bouncing off the bathroom tiles drown it all out- the sorrow and the sound of sorrow. I'm starting to wonder the same about rainstorms, perhaps they have the same magical power. It's like the falling trees in the forest; if no one hears you, maybe that means you're not crying your heart out at all. Perhaps that means you're actually happy in that universe where tears are uncountable and unperceived and unheard.

They say that a butterfly can flap its wings and cause a tornado halfway across the world. This is just a romanticized way to say that the smallest insignificant factors can change the course of our lives and can turn calm into a storm. That small, insignificant moment for me was when I held a stranger's eyes that one second too long, on a beach somewhere on the Indian Ocean. One second we were strangers and the next, the sun was rising, a literal tequila sunrise if you will. Syrupy grenadine reds and oranges and streaks of pink. I had sand in every crease of that cotton dress you loved so much. One second was enough to put me here stomach-up on the grass in Jardin des Tuileries. When I should have been admiring the Monets nearby in the kind of outfit that can only be worn in the City of Light. One second is what made me drink almost an entire bottle of Beaujolais at lunch. I was sitting outside before the rain at our favorite table at that unpronounceable place on Rue des Rosiers with the wobbly wicker chairs all facing the street. The best seat in town to watch life unfold, you would say to me, between drags of your hand-rolled cigarette. I hated your smoking, but I loved your old soul. How you would scribble French poetry on pieces of paper that you kept in your pockets and would eventually end up running after when they slipped out, inevitably flying away with the wind. I used to laugh, as you grasped violently at the air at the little elusive paper squares that said things like corps de femme, collines blanches, and cuisses blanches. Somehow, I convinced myself that smoking, poetry, and old souls were inseparable. I should have known that one vice leads to many.

I should have known that even the people we think belong to us are just strangers that we let into our lives and write into our narrative, thinking that we know the character enough to plan the next chapters. But we can never know. A character is fictional, they exist as we want them to, as we create them in our minds, and at a certain point in the book, you turn the page, and they deceive you. From one punctuation point to the next, they reveal their flaws. Like when you arrive at his five-floor walk-up in the Marais on a Monday afternoon, unexpected. I keep going back to the one second it took to turn the key and find him there inside my linen bed sheets and inside someone who wasn't me. And I stood wordless like the fool that I was as I thought about that one damned second too long, that extra second, all the months before, on a beach on the Indian Ocean when I held his gaze, and he mouthed, "Bonsoir."

That was the butterfly, and this, this is the natural disaster.

The Letter R

What language do they fuck each other in? Does she whisper, "vieni amore," in that fleeting moment the French call la petite mort? Throw her head back in ecstasy, awaken a living revenant every morning on his side of the bed? She sometimes wonders these things, these irrational, stupid, immensely unimportant things. Turning them over in her head like a smooth stone held in a calm, contemplative, as if somehow the answer will change something. As if knowing will fill that empty, dark space that exists somewhere under her ribcage, wedged up against her heart. It won't, and she knows it. People talk about getting over someone as if it were a physics assignment to be completed, a household item to check off a grocery list.

Cherries. Check. Toilet paper. Check. Forget him. Check. Erase the last year. Check. What they don't realize is you're trying to move on without looking back and seeing the sun glint off her long black hair, her manicured hand fitting in his better than yours ever did, ever will, ever would or ever hope to. In your rear-view mirror is a perfect picture, the objects closer and farther than they might appear, the only thing that's distorted is that you're not in it. She loathes that girl and her perfect everything, the way the Roman alphabet rolls off her tongue with such fucking ease, the reverberating double consonants and all those other beautiful sounds that don't exist in the English language. The sounds themselves are pure seduction, they can't help themselves, they pull you in. Beckoning.

You are almost compelled to put your mouth on a mouth like hers. Need to know what makes those words sound so good, what it feels like. What a tongue like that could do when it's wrapped around something other than the letter R. So she can't blame him for leaving. He was right to want to know the answers to these questions, he was right to keep asking the questions. The perché, the why is irrelevant. The wanting and the needing to know all those foreign tongues. This is what predominates over the reason, over reason.

Pompeii

My dad passed away almost two weeks ago. Another soldier lost in the seemingly bleak battle against what has appropriately been called "the emperor of all maladies." Without timelines, I had booked the week of Ferragosto to go back to visit. Not knowing it would be the last six days I would spend with him in this life. We had been riding the roller-coaster of Stage Four colorectal cancer for almost two-and-a-half years. The immediate stomach-drop upon discovery and thinking he had weeks, not months. To the surprising recovery post-surgery and post-radiation that saw him regain a startling 30 pounds and cross the Atlantic to walk me down the aisle. It was in May this year that a steadily decreasing weight and appetite led to the discovery of a recurrence and a terminal diagnosis.

We were heartbroken, and I was an ocean away. But God is kind and gave us time together. I spent entire days watching my dad breathe, this tiny human swaddled in blankets. All sharp angles, and bone cushioned by a plethora of pillows positioned here and there. I fed him ice cream and washed his face, our parent-child roles in the distorted reversal that age and illness inevitably bring. This ultimately puts you face-to-face with the intrinsic, interwoven nature of living and dying. My dad died in the morning on a Sunday. The night before, he waved a little goodbye to me. The gesture of a kid, bending and unbending four fingers of the hand- up and down, up and down. It was the most he could do as he was no longer able to talk. I replay that simple motion in my head like a favorite scene from a movie. It has been said that cancer puts emphasis on the dying rather death itself. I agree. Towards the end, it is like being forced to watch Pompeii in slow-motion with no means to intervene or to look away and at a certain point, at the height of suffering, almost hopeful for the final explosion and finally, ashes and slow-burning ember. The ashes of a person typically weigh four pounds when all is said and done. I carried my dad's for a brief moment at the cemetery, close to my chest. I couldn't help but think about all those nights I would fall asleep on the couch as a child, and he would carry me so carefully up to my bed. A balancing act of blankets and teddy bears. At one point in life, we will all carry one another.

Moscow Mules

I once knew a boy who hated his name, he was Russian and had come to live in my city when he was six. Linguists say often say that six is the age that determines whether or not you'll speak more than one language without the hint of an accent. The second language has to be learned before that. Nikolai that was his name. Nikolai had one that was barely detectable, but I could always see the extra bit of effort that he put into each and every English word to make sure it stayed that way. I have always loved the idea of something foreign and was immediately drawn to him because of his name. He would often answer phone calls from his parents a safe distance away from other people. This was so we wouldn't hear the sounds of the Cyrillic alphabet streaming from his lips.

Russian, to me, is an impossible language to describe because it is both smooth and sharp all at once. I was entranced by this concept and contemporarily by the boy. I started learning the language, spending hours perfecting my calligraphy and dreaming of sunsets in St. Petersburg. When I was twenty, I rode the railway from China through Russia. The days and nights were blurring into each other, with the fluidity of watercolors. I read Dostoevsky and drank vodka from dirty, smudged glasses that had probably never left the train cabins in their entire lives. The day we arrived in his small town, I stepped off the train and thought about the smallness of the world and about where we end up and where we come from. I thought about staying there forever. Somewhere in the middle of Siberia where finally everything would be foreign, meaning my wandering soul might finally stop waking me up in the middle of the night. But then the train whistle blew, and I hurried back on. Somehow, I knew that there were more adventures awaiting, but I still think of that moment and of him whenever I drink a Moscow Mule. The sting of the ginger lingering on my tongue.

Small Towns and Big Dreams

She's beautiful, I'll give you that. The kind of girl you might describe as acqua e sapone. That's how Italians refer to the girl-next-door type of beauty, soap, and water. It's the kind of beauty that gets on your nerves if you're like me and can't bear to leave the house without a perfect jet-black cat's eye. You always had a thing for blondes anyways, and even though boys might tell you they don't have a type, they do. All my years of dating have taught me this. My ex-boyfriends are all with girls that look exactly like their first loves which makes me wonder, is love ever lost or are we just on an eternal journey to find a replacement for the one that got away?

We met in high school in small town America, you playing the perfect role of a foreign exchange student and me, just one of the many girls that fell for you and your dark hair. Your dark hair that would fall over your eyes in calculus, you and your leather jacket and All-Stars. The way you'd ask questions by inflecting the end of your sentences rather than invert the subject. You and your natural drop-dead gorgeous smile. Everyone knew you were leaving after graduation, back to a small Italian town that no one could pronounce and you'd just tell people it was near Milan because it was the only city we knew. It's pointless, my friends told me, he'll just break your heart. What do you expect? He's Italian, that's what they do. Plus, the first week after becoming official Facebook friends, all the girls in the senior year had seen the one in your pictures and by the casual drape of her arm around your neck and the way you looked at her baby blues, it was undeniable she was the girlfriend you'd left behind waiting for you. Basically, we knew how this story would end before it started, and I started it anyways by saying yes when you asked me out after your first soccer game. It was a brisk September night under the stadium lights. You had just scored the winning goal and ran straight up to me, sweaty and exuberant and probably full of the adrenaline-induced confidence that you needed to cheat on a girl an ocean away. It was a teenage dream. I just couldn't say no though, despite my head, and it wasn't to make everyone jealous or to prove my friends wrong or any of a million reasons It was just the way you looked at me as if you had to have me. And so it was. It was autumn afternoons skipping class, the slivers of golden light in your eyes, my cheeks blushed from the cold and from you; then it was Christmas with candy cane kisses (you had never had one before), and I made you wear red flannel shirts, and you told me that America felt like home, as you strung rainbow lights around me and I tried to convince myself that you would stay forever. They say that it takes four seasons to fall in love with someone truly, but I fell for you the very first. I wanted this to be a different high school romance, but as all the good ones do, ours ended with a prom night promise and a flight to Italy in the morning that I wasn't on. I've moved since then, you probably knew that. You always said that the town was too small for me, but you were wrong, I left because I couldn't escape the memory of you that haunts all my favorite places, I needed new areas untouched by you. Actually, I needed a new you because the last time I checked, I saw that you're back with her and sometimes I think maybe you always were.

The Way We Were

You're sitting there, and I'm sitting here, and we're sharing the same space, the same air, and that's about it. I keep thinking about how we got here, to this dead-end destination that we had promised each other we'd never end up in. We were the golden couple, the ones that everyone envied. I know, that's what women in my position always say, but I swear it's the truth. I'm not trying to paint a perfect picture of the past, my memory isn't distorted even though our relationship is.

We were that couple in the restaurant--ankles crossed, elbows on the table and noses almost touching--meeting in the middle. We always used to meet in the middle, and now you refuse to move from your hypothetical side, even a hypothetical half-centimeter. If you had seen us, you'd have seen a raven-haired, thirty-something-dreamer with fire in her eyes. Throwing her head back in the kind of pure agony, only the most real form of laughter can give you. You'd have seen him and known that he was the jock back in high school, but not the kind that never left the hallways. The kind that ran with that natural charisma all the way to New York City and became a restaurateur in Greenwich. The kind of man that orders a 1996 Barolo on a regular Tuesday night to celebrate living.

What happened to him?

What of the dreamer?

And where did the celebrating go?

It's magnificently unsettling to be sharing a surname with a stranger, the only thing we've had in common for the year. I hate myself for thinking these thoughts, for giving up on the way we were. But then again, resentment feeds on resentment, and somehow that's the only sentiment we seem to cultivate.

Resentment and anger. They work a bit like emotional heroin, you know that they are toxic and yet you can't stop, you need that fix over and over again, and you'll stop at nothing to get it.

Sometimes, I'll catch myself observing him out of the corner of my eye and for a millisecond, I recognize him again. It's usually when he's doing something banal, so ordinary that no one would ever notice it. Like when he obsessively touches his right earlobe while on the telephone. At that moment, my brain plays tricks on me, and my automatic, unconscious response is to smile.

And just for a moment, I'm smiling, and he's tugging his stupid ear-lobe, and we are the way we were.

Magnolias in Milan

It was spring when we met. The panna cotta colored magnolias were in full bloom in Milan, and their sweet perfume seemed to come in waves, in little puffs of perfection. He paused and looked up at them for a moment, almost pink against the bright, bluebird sky, but then instantly regretted stopping. She used to love this time of year. Primavera. If she had been here now, holding his arm on the way to nowhere, she would have undoubtedly commented on the magnolias.

Flowers are a fickle thing, they are there in beginnings and endings and loyal to neither.

He thought back to the beginning, eight years ago that seemed like a lifetime and a second all at once. It was a Wednesday evening. He was in the classic mid-week rut, wishing he hadn't already told his friends he'd be at aperitivo after work. The isolation of his apartment and a solitary Nastro Azzurro on the couch with the game on was tempting. But one of his pet peeves was canceling at the last minute, so he begrudgingly buttoned his trench, popped the collar against the light breeze and headed off towards Piazza Duomo. As he passed his reflection in the Prada window front, he took stock of his reflection. Tall, broad-shouldered, young enough to still be reckless on occasion. Light brown hair a little too messy to pass for being intentional. Hazel eyes that his carta d'identità decided to call "Verde", and a 5 o'clock shadow that already looked like he hadn't shaved in days. No, he didn't look classically Italian, and the only thing that gave him away was his perfectly pressed blue shirt and leather shoes. As an art director, he was used to curating beauty. It was probably his downfall because beauty is always evolving, and so were his girlfriends, to satisfy the peaks and valleys of a life inundated by beautiful things. Sometimes he blamed it on Italy as well, he was surrounded by beauty. If you don't stop in your tracks to admire one church, you'll just as easily find another, more stunning, a few blocks on. At least this is what he always believed until that Wednesday evening in primavera when he saw her.

She wasn't classically beautiful, she was like that first church that you could walk by in hopes of finding a better one. Especially in a town like Milan. Thinking about it now, it was something about her that was indefinable, a combination of things, a chemical equation that resulted in alchemy. Her long, dark hair was falling down her back as she laughed hysterically, her head thrown back as if she were laughing at God, her leather glove clad-hand gripping a book that he couldn't make out. He would later discover it was a copy of The Unbearable Lightness of Being. Had he known how this would all turn out, he would have realized that the book was a sign. Yet, as so many men before him in history, a glance was enough. A laugh was all it took. He was entranced, spellbound by her presence. Not by her literal presence but how she was present like no other woman he had ever known. She was living in the moment he saw her across the via, not only existing like many of us are. She was exuberant, radiant, and real. She made him want to live.

Those words were the beginning, and strangely also the end if read with the end in mind. She made him want to live. And so he left.

Wander(lust)

I am happily committed, don't get me wrong. He is my kindred spirit, the kind of man that I always wanted for myself. And yet.

And yet do you ever see someone and just know that if things were different, if you were different, you could be together?

Sometimes I envision how it would be, this illicit affair. I wouldn't dare make the first move, I'm not one for that. No, he'd have to do it. It would be inevitable because we've been eye fucking each other since the moment we met. It's gotten to the point where I have to avert my gaze when I walk into a room. To avoid catching his and then having to carry around the guilt of how much it affects me for the rest of the day. His eyes are dark, like mine. It's probably already a bad sign, I've always been afraid of the dark and what they do to me, it scares me. They are dark brown, framed by even darker lashes and I thank my lucky stars when he comes in wearing sunglasses.

For a split-second, I'm saved. He's all wrong for me, and anyway, he's had a girlfriend for ages, since puberty I imagine. At times, I think about how they are together, a pastime that does nothing more than feed my insatiable imagination. I want to find ourselves in a situation where there is nowhere to run to. No excuses to not do what we're thinking about. I've always wanted one of those moments where the lights turn off, and the main characters look at each other and you, as the spectator, can see that this is it, they have to give in to temptation.

Like the pull of gravity, like the tides, there is no other alternative and no other direction to move in except into each other. Perhaps this is what they mean by wanderlust. That it was never about places in the first place, it was always about people.

Acknowledgements:

I would like to thank my mother who is a living example that you can never be overeducated or overdressed. She is the reason I was able to travel extensively growing up and she let me fill every corner of the house (and at times her own luggage) with books, thus nurturing my love of reading and writing. Next, I have to thank my grandma for all the struggles she faced and overcame as an immigrant to Canada. When I find myself in a difficult situation as a foreigner in Italy, I remember that she once experienced the same and I am able to persevere. A huge thank you to my little brother Jordan who has shown me how to keep on dancing, no matter what life brings. Ai miei suoceri, grazie di farmi sentire a casa in Italia. Thank you to Adil and the entire Leaf Publishing House team for making this childhood dream of mine to publish a book a beautiful reality and to Ara Chi Jung for the meticulous editing and advice. And finally, grazie di cuore to my husband Massimiliano, for turning my own story into nothing short of a fairy tale.

CPSIA information can be obtained
at www.ICGtesting.com
Printed in the USA
BVHW070503020720
582659BV00006B/262